Additional praise for
*Skirmishes on the Okie-Irish Border*

Maureen Oehler DuRant's poetry collection, *Skirmishes on the Okie-Irish Border,* reveals the fault lines of family, culture, and class, and, in her intimate series "Sonnets from the Marriage-Impaired," the struggles of maintaining a marriage with a military spouse. DuRant composes equally well in form and in free verse, engaging readers' attention and admiration from the first poem to the last.

—Jeanetta Calhoun Mish, Oklahoma State Poet Laureate and author of *What I Learned at the War*

In contrast to the Irish poet William Butler Yeats' famous charge to poets, the poems in Maureen Oehler DuRant's debut collection look with a warm eye—not to mention a playful, gently satiric, and at times self-deprecating wit—on life, the sorties of the author's titular heritage, the various pleasures of small-box discount stores, and, especially, the tidal ebb and flow of love and marriage. These are poems of detailed invention, precise observation, painstaking craft, and great charm.

—John Morris, author of *Noise and Stories*

Maureen DuRant's *Skirmishes* is filled with energy. The language throbs. Memories cringe then recoil into courage. Daily experiences bounce off each other with vibrant, skeptic insight. Her poetic range includes marriage, children, heritage, even war—all with a persistent voice defining feminine space in a borderland too familiar to be ignored.

—Ken Hada, author of *Not Quite Pilgrims*

# Skirmishes
## on the
# Okie-Irish Border

Poems

Maureen Oehler DuRant

Press 53
*Winston-Salem*

Press 53, LLC
PO Box 30314
Winston-Salem, NC 27130

First Edition

Copyright © 2020 by Maureen Oehler DuRant

All rights reserved, including the right of reproduction in whole or in part in any form except in the case of brief quotations embodied in critical articles or reviews. For permission, contact publisher at editor@Press53.com, or at the address above.

Cover Photo, "Mossy," by author

Author Photo by BD DuRant

Cover design by Christopher Forrest and Kevin Morgan Watson

Library of Congress Control Number
2020934176

Printed on acid-free paper
ISBN 978-1-950413-23-2

for BD,
my battle buddy

Many thanks to the editors of the following publications, where versions of these poems first appeared:

*Crosstimbers,* "Cursed"

*The Great American Wise Ass Poetry Anthology,* "Talking in My Sleep"

*Proud to Be: Writing by American Warriors,* "Rolling Along"

*Red River Review,* "Help Never Arrives at the Dollar General in Medicine Park"

*Westview,* "Family Ties"

To my editor, Christopher Forrest, for the long hours he devoted to this project and his never-ending patience. Additional thanks to Kevin Morgan Watson and Press 53 for providing *Skirmishes* a wonderful home.

I am grateful for the many teachers who have mentored me along the way: to Cathy Smith Bowers, a woman who loves a laugh and an abiding image; to Morri Creech, who believes in form and his students; to John Morris, a professor exemplar with a great big laugh.

To my family. To my mom who left Belfast, Northern Ireland to marry an American soldier from Broken Bow, Oklahoma. To my dad who loved my mom. To my sister, Helen Oehler Rollins who always shows up. To my mother-in-law, Miriam Brown DuRant who listened to me read poems and taught me what grows on her farm.

To my son, Colin, who makes me laugh even though he isn't interested in my poems.

To my husband, Brian David DuRant, always, forever and ever, amen.

# Contents

| | |
|---|---|
| *'Tis a Silly Place* | 3 |
| Skirmishes | 4 |
| My Garden of Hopeful, yet Low Expectations | 5 |
| Family Ties | 6 |
| Made Up | 8 |
| Sonnets from the Marriage-Impaired: <br>    Don't Tell Me to Smile | 9 |
| Keeping My Head above Water | 10 |
| Presto. Change-o. Hobo. | 11 |
| Master of Fear | 12 |
| Sonnets from the Marriage-Impaired: <br>    Give until It Hurts | 13 |
| The Farm's Physical Remains | 14 |
| Bad Fences Make Good Marriages | 15 |
| I ♥ Men | 16 |
| Ancestry.com | 18 |
| Sonnets from the Marriage-Impaired: <br>    Keep Secrets | 19 |
| Freshman Biology Lab Test | 20 |
| Snake in the Grass | 21 |
| Sonnets from the Marriage-Impaired: <br>    Play Fair | 22 |
| Help Never Arrives at the Dollar General <br>    in Medicine Park | 23 |
| Bad Blood | 24 |
| Sonnets from the Marriage-Impaired: <br>    Eat at Your Own Table | 25 |
| Casualties of War | 26 |
| Something Comes and Takes What We Don't Want | 27 |
| Battlefield Photographs | 28 |
| Work | 30 |
| Sonnets from the Marriage-Impaired: <br>    Share Troubles | 31 |
| Petty Thefts | 32 |
| Hello, Leave a Message | 33 |
| *Rolling Along* | 34 |
| Sonnets from the Marriage-Impaired: <br>    Take Your Time | 35 |
| The Elephant in the War | 36 |

| | |
|---|---|
| Limits to Human Curiosities | 37 |
| Persistent Suicide | 38 |
| I knew better | 39 |
| Eye Exam | 40 |
| *Excuse me, Mister Rooster Hat, you've crossed the line* | 41 |
| Lost in First Class | 42 |
| Sonnets from the Marriage-Impaired: Spend Time Together | 43 |
| Local Traffic | 44 |
| Love-Hate Contract | 45 |
| The Magically Lucky Ones | 46 |
| *O, Mothers, Where Art Thou?* | 47 |
| Volunteers | 48 |
| The Curse | 49 |
| Dress for Success | 50 |
| Still Life | 51 |
| Sonnets from the Marriage-Impaired: Answer to Many Names | 52 |
| *Gone to America* | 53 |
| How I Learned American History | 54 |
| For the Pie-Anxious on Thanksgiving | 55 |
| I Believe All the Marys | 56 |
| Happy Birthday, Dear Helen | 57 |
| Weathered Men | 58 |
| Sometimes We Remember What's Hard to Forget | 59 |
| *Fine* | 60 |
| The Cuckoo Order of Birds | 61 |
| No Escape from the Good Deed of the Day | 62 |
| There's this | 63 |
| Fighters Fight | 64 |
| Arrangements | 66 |
| Toasted on Toasts with the Good Stuff | 68 |
| Sonnets from the Marriage-Impaired: Cease Fires before You Say What Can't Be Forgotten | 70 |
| Escape Routes Wait in the Woods | 71 |
| About the Author | 73 |

*One of the damnable things about it was that you couldn't take sides. You couldn't take sides.*
—Derek Mahon

Skirmishes on the Okie-Irish Border

## 'Tis a Silly Place

Last night, it would seem, a storm
swept the sisal welcome mat
from the porch and I can't find the paper.
A pot of pansies is broken, but the flowers
still smile up at me like little drunken clowns
sleeping off too many cocktails
decorated with tiny umbrellas.

# Skirmishes

Before I was let loose on the street to play,
to wander the sidewalk on Woodvale Road,
and find a girl my size to be my friend, my ma
told me how to answer the question, *What are ya,
Catholic or Protestant?* So, when the kids circled
me, I offered each a Jelly Baby from the bag
my Aunt Norah bought me at the sweet shop
across from the Belfast Blitz site where I stood
and cried because my ma told me about her friend
who died and the German bomb dropped on the roof
of their house on Israel Street. So my granny took
the whole lot of them across the road to another house
and there they stayed even after the other family
came home. That's what they got for leaving.

When the biggest boy, whose name was Devlin,
asked, I gave my answer: *I'm American.*
*What kind of American?* he demanded and I said,
*The Oklahoma kind.* Then the kids started
whooping it up like fake Indians on *The Lone Ranger,*
asking me if I lived in a teepee, rode a horse, been scalped?
*I live in a normal house, you stupid eejits!*
The circling stopped. Devlin put out his hand.
*Give me your candy.* I belted "The Wild Rover,"
*No. Nay. Never,* clutched the white twisted sack,
and stood my ground on the Okie-Irish border.

# My Garden of Hopeful, yet Low Expectations

Come spring I plant rows of tomatoes,
hairy twigs that leave a bitter scent
on my fingers. Conceived in eastern
greenhouses, the seedlings promise fruit
disguised as vegetables. Wire cages
and blankets of pine straw shield yellow
blossoms on tender shoots. And each year,
late chills prick the night with deadly spears
leaving few survivors who offer
communion for swarms of locusts that follow.

# Family Ties

Refused to sit down,
Miss High and Mighty.
My Oklahoma aunts
told the story again and again.
Jack's girl don't know her people.
Twisting on my new white
summer Keds, my cotton
sundress wilting in the heat,
I crossed my arms against
the smell of grease, a heavy
weight like red earth refusing
to scrub away or a tick
on a coon hound, ready to burst.
The magnolia wallpaper,
faded and peeling, exposed layers
of stained plywood, wadded
pages of magazines stuffed
in cracks, trying to keep
dust and vermin at bay.
A fan stuttered at the end
of each turn, stirring old
catalogs stacked
on an enamel table, weighted
by bottles and sticky glasses.
I mumbled, *Nice to meet
you.* Ruth cackled, her empty
gums opening a soft cave,
her watery gray eyes,
shriveled beads in swollen
sockets, repaid my gaze,
recognizing kin.
Lurching from her kitchen
chair, she pressed her face
close to mine and I smelled
her familiar breath.
She reached out and pinched
my arm, twisting
my tanned skin, digging
yellow nails into flesh.

I ran, the screen door slammed—
red dogs in the hard dirt
yard raised their jowled heads.
I waited in my daddy's
Buick, borrowed for the road
trip into the Ouachita Mountains.
The sweat trickled down
my face and the welt raised.

My aunts were wrong. I knew
my people. I knew the glove
box hid a flask of Southern Comfort.
I knew Daddy winking, swigging
a long draw, then coaxing *Just a taste,
baby girl*. The bitter taste of poteen,
the fleeting warmth of rotgut,
and the lingering spirits left marks:
eyes the color of Bigfork chert, soft
teeth, a loose laugh, and a whiskey want.

# Made Up

The mortician drained you and laid you out
in the crepe, mauve dress worn only once
to a granddaughter's wedding. A beauty
school dropout, it would seem, has given you
a makeover. Hair left in Toni stiff spirals,
frosty blue eyeshadow, Siren Scarlet lips,
make you look, as you would say, like
an old whore saddled up to a dank bar
in a one-horse town. A duo of daughters
go to work. I zip open your cosmetic bag,
an Avon lady's gift with purchase and find
your face. Pond's cold cream on cotton pads
swipe away the make-up death mask.
Helen dusts your nose with Estee Lauder's
translucent powder and I draw your Tabu
lips, blot on a folded tissue. A boar's hair
bristle brush loosens the stiff curls
into your soft gray waves, summer storm
clouds threatening games of jump rope,
skipping over the spinning length
of clothesline stolen from the neighbor's
yard. A tisket, a tasket, my mom
is in her casket. I twist the lipstick tube again,
line my mouth in the color that called me home.

Sonnets from the Marriage-Impaired:
  Don't Tell Me to Smile

You chide me for a frown, a down-turned lip
that fixes on my face in nothing thoughts.
A few to-dos: plans for our weekend trip,
lamb chops for dinner, soaking out the spots,
a sauce on your blue button-down work shirt.
You want smiles. The deep elevens between
brows cause consternation, what wrong, what hurt
do I suffer? Where must you intervene?
My husband, I wish my face were frozen
like Mona Lisa's hanging in the Louvre
or Goya's Isabel. You have chosen
to love flesh. Trust me. Trust me that it's true.
My scowl is only to say the sky is gray,
not to hang in museums, forever on display.

## Keeping My Head above Water

A woman from across the street, somewhere
down the road, near the ocean, I don't know
where, screams. Last night—no—early this morning,
the clock glowed 3:00 AM, still dark when she
cried, her shrills coming in waves, madness
of some kind: *Let me go. Let me go.*
*Let me go.* I startled, then coming awake knew
it was her. I waited before closing
the sliding glass door to the balcony
that overlooks the road where she wanders
sometimes in the day, yelling and pointing
at carpenters mending fences or men
trimming trees: *You can't do that. You can't*
*do that.* In the pauses that fill her lungs
to fuel the cries, the surf seems to calm her,
the break to shore soothes, but then she shrieks
again: *Let me go.* I want to reach out,
hold the hand that accuses the empty
air. But she is strong and I am scared she
could pull me under with her, so I slide
the glass door shut, grope my way back to bed,
twist my body into a closed, curved shell,
and sink into a sleep that drowns the noise.

Presto. Change-o. Hobo.

My harried mother
transformed me:
brown eye shadow dirt
smudged across my face,
torn dungarees,
Dad's old felt hat,
a bandana bindle tied to a stick.

My posse of girl pals: two
fairy princesses—crowns
bobby pinned in place—
a Dallas Cowboy cheerleader,
two brides without grooms,
one mini-Madonna, and me
trolled the streets for Pixie
Sticks, Milk Duds, Mrs. Murphy's
pennies, and popcorn balls
Dad wrapped in waxed paper.

My friends teetered on plastic heels,
lagged, stopped to pull up
socks, sat on curbs to rest, reapplied
Bonnie Bell lip gloss.
Cold in acetate lace,
the princesses and brides
went home early, plastic
pumpkins half empty.
The cheerleader scraped
her knee after a cartwheel,
spilled her sweets and gave in.
Madonna ran off with a Batman.

Blocks from home, I tramped
to stoops, the toes cut
out of last year's boots,
knocking on doors, demanding
my due. My pillowcase
grew heavy with loot,
sweat dampened my brother's
borrowed work shirt,
"Billy" stitched over my heart.

Master of Fear


On Thursday nights, the Vaska on Ferris Avenue
played scary movies. For a dollar, money earned
babysitting, I sat with friends rocking red velveteen
seats as Hollywood schooled us in horror: *Halloween*
again and again, whirring chainsaws, lost boy vampires,
suburban houses whispering warnings, nightmares of fire
ruined Freddy. In perfect unison, we screamed at Hitch-
cock's lessons: blackbirds swooping—pecking plumage,
the pulsing shower scene montage. King exposed
pets gone mad. Danny's REDRUM, REDRUM raised goose
bumps on bare, perfect flesh. *Carrie* played the night I mastered
fear. A boy I liked sat next to me, shared my armrest, passed
me a box of Junior Mints. We watched the crazy mother hit
the girl, repeating: *Eve was weak. Say it.* I ate the cool mints
one at a time letting the chocolate melt on my tongue. He slipped
his hand up my school skirt, fumbling in the dark. I knew I
should push it away, tell him to stop. But I kept eating
the candy, staring at the screen, wanting to feel good and afraid.

# Sonnets from the Marriage-Impaired:
## Give until It Hurts

In this sonnet, not Portuguese, but mine,
I do declare, for our love, I would kill.
Just how do I love you? Most all the time?
I would give you a kidney. If you still
needed my other organs, they'd be yours.
I will pee in one of those bags, carry
it like a purse. If it happens the cures
for your other ails—the capillary
crap that roadblocks blood to your gasping heart,
the discs in your back that bulge, or an eye
that blinds—need my body, take flesh apart
piece by piece to make you whole. Should I die
giving you it all, live resurrected
knowing death and love rise unexpected.

# The Farm's Physical Remains

Back beyond the pecan tree
that stands like an ancient guard
to the old pasture, a dump—
grown over with muscadine
vines—offers clues: blue bottles,
waves of metal roofs, and chain.

## Bad Fences Make Good Marriages

Hurricane Matthew took down the back fence.
That's not a metaphor.

Before the storm, the planks of pine wavered.
Streaked with swashes of algae, freckled

with flakes of mold, the boards' top ends
warped and jagged like the teeth of a seven-year-old

or an old dude who both smile anyway—no shame
in the gaps—it stood security for poinsettias

hanging on long after the Christmas parties,
playthings found on the beach: a baby doll head,

a My Little Pony, and a Happy Meal Minion.
Tiny perfect ferns grew in its corners,

spawned, I guess, from spores floating in the wind
or pooped there by a grackle. The fence, at best, formed

a precarious barrier and we both knew its time was up.
Yet after the fall, after we returned to our island from exile,

you propped it up again, wired the wood together
with coat hangers, vertical and hopeful till the next big squall.

# I ♥ Men

The man who delivers our propane says
he looks to cold months because he knows
he'll drive up our steep hill and fill my tank
every week or so. He says I'm the prettiest
woman in Comanche County and pumps
in the gas. Full of it, but I love him.
I love his uniform, Greg—embroidered
in cursive right on the spot his hand rests
when he pledges allegiance.
I also love the guy in my spin class
who rides the bike next to mine. He mouths, *let's
do this* and winks. I stand in the saddle
and race him up the hills, pump the pedals
hard. I love his spandex shorts, tie in front,
his No-Shave November lumberjack look,
his cocky dismount when the workout ends.
There's an old man at Brookridge Extended
Care I also love. Every day, he sits
in death's anteroom bent over
a cardboard box of jigsaw. I love his
sad hairy ears, flip-flops, the thick glasses
he wears at the end of his nose. Every
week or so he calls me over as I'm
hauling a plastic basket of Aunt Sue's
dirty laundry. He hands me the last piece.
I complete the picture: The Orient
Express, a Tiki hut on a desert
island, and one time, a pinup—nude but
for the heels and book. A female
Holden Caulfield, I fall half in love
with every man I meet. I fell half in love with you
on a winter night in a bar when you offered
to hold my coat. *I'll keep it safe*, you said. *Ready.*

You drank pints of ale, thumbed a paperback
copy of *The Call of the Wild*, kept score
on the Cowboys game, my red wool double-
breasted coat folded on the barstool next
to you. I danced with almost all the guys
there, took in the smell of Old Spice, Brut,
mouthwash, whiskey, leather, and clean white
T-shirts. But at last call, you held my coat up,
I dropped my arms into the sleeves, and I
knew you held the other half of love, slipped
on my shoulders in one swift maneuver.

# Ancestry.com

The spit I swabbed from inside my cheek, buccal
cells spun in a lab, spat back: 92 percent
Irish Marys and Johns. The rest?
Some Viking raider I would guess. Erik
or Leif on an excursion, raping
and pillaging, his seed left to splinter
into my 8 percent Norse, just enough
to feel the berserker I keep in chains.
I know the women in my family, Marys
who might welcome a weary wanderer,
offer him a cup of tea and a bun,
her husband at the pub as usual
squandering wages on pints of Guinness,
stumbling home to claim his turf and his brood
who dodge punches and scatter to the streets,
all except the wee one who punches back.

## Sonnets from the Marriage-Impaired:
### Keep Secrets

Mornings, over the coffee and paper, you report
my nightly conversations, my unconscious words
muttered in bed. You, posing as friend-of-the-court,
give testimony, "Last evening, my wife said, *'Birds
in the house mean death is on the way.'*" I sigh, start
to explain, and the toast snaps up. "Just two nights
ago, my wife whispered, *'Hands to yourself or sit apart'*"
Eggs sputter in the skillet, yolks swirled into the whites.
Now a game you love, monitoring nocturnal sounds,
my declarations. *I like you both; it's a toss-up!*
You, tuned in like a tired FBI agent waiting for grounds
to prosecute, eavesdropping on private, juicy gossip,
listen closely to my advice: Go to sleep. Long ago
I stumbled. Don't learn what you do not want to know.

# Freshman Biology Lab Test

The professor set microscopes in rows,
slid slides under lenses. To take the test,
students stooped, squinted into eyepieces,
recorded answers. A proctor wore
a silver whistle like a referee
and every forty-five seconds, he blew.
We stretched, picked up our half-sheets of copy
paper and moved. Slide. Slide. Slide. Fourteen times
in a row, I printed in the blank space:
STRIATED MUSCLE TISSUE. For weeks, I
flipped flashcards, memorized parts of the cells:
centriole, mitochondrion, Golgi;
and a few epithelial tissues: proc
simple cuboidal, stratified squamous,:
pseudostratified columnar. But, when
I twisted the fine focus adjustment
and the coarse focus, cells just blurred and swirled
into pretty pink and white waves, sticky
cotton candy on pointy paper cones.

## Snake in the Grass

Along with a half-gallon of Blue Bell,
a bag of Flamin' Hot Cheetos,
and a six pack of Oklahoma 3.2 beer,
I bought every last snake
in the toy aisle at Dollar General.
Darren, the late night checker,
lifted each rubber serpent
from my red shopping basket,
held it up by the tail, and like a curator
of reptiles at the zoo, gave a tour
to me and the guy who stopped
in for a pack of Lucky Strikes
and a diet Mountain Dew.
*Common Adder, shy fella,*
*but he'll bite if you bother him.*
*Black Rat, you want that one,*
*eats mice; keeps vermin away.*
*Coral, some poison, some not.*
*Red and black, friend of Jack.*
*Red and yella, kills a fella*
*And here's your Diamondback.*
Darren whistled, glanced at my ring,
shook the silent rattle, dropped it
in the plastic sack with the receipt.
For a joke, I scattered my catch
on the front steps, discovered
the tan ones glowed fluorescent yellow
under the porch light, arranged
a few in a snake pit diorama
on the Welcome! mat and left
you this note: *The one that hisses is real.*

# Sonnets from the Marriage-Impaired:
## Play Fair

Eyes closed, lurching like a child
at a birthday party pinning the tail
on the donkey, I reach, fingers wild,
to feel your face, your breathing braille.
You asked me, could I recognize you
by touch? Trip along a lineup, choose?
Your nose, slick with night's oily dew,
your chin's deep crevice—a 3D tattoo,
eyes like Michelangelo's David chiseled
from a marble block, lips curved, a quick
grin. You lead my fingers to twisted bristle
that trails from your chest to your prick,
all revealed in my man, the ass I always knew
manipulates our games, obstructs my view.

## Help Never Arrives at the Dollar General in Medicine Park

*Price check* bleats Rita into her micro-
phone, her words sucked through wires
into a loud speaker that inhales the pleading

call and spits out scratchy nonsense
where it floats into aisles overflowing
with boxes of generic groceries (instant

coffee, potted meat, Jiffy Cornbread Mix),
yard art (bug-eyed bullfrogs squatting
on sticks, neon pink daises in plastic pots),

and crates of Shasta while a woman
stands juggling baloney, a bag of Ranch
Doritos, a six-pack of Kool-Aid, a box

of Kraft macaroni and powdered cheese,
a pregnancy test (Accurate! Plus Appears
for Positive!), and a baby on her hip,

sleeping—thumb his mouth, fine ringlets
plastered against a flushed face—next
to a blue fairy tattoo smiling on her shoulder.

# Bad Blood

Again on my American
trek into "Who am I?" my
ancestors give me the finger
from the wherever-they-are-place,
surely not in Heaven, seated at the right hand.

To date on my dashed DAR
hope-and-dream: a grandfather
tried in Paul's Valley for shooting
out the eye of a town pioneer
and his horse (*Why, the poor nag,
Grandpa?*), two Confederate
deserters (*And who would blame them?*
my sister asks), and many men
gone missing, one to Quebec,
never to be seen again.

Last night a trail unraveled,
a last road to take. My heart
quickened, here is Mary Jane Watts,
back, back, back, to Salem.
To a wronged cousin whom I could
mourn? Standing with the descendants
of the accused? Demanding justice
and an edict to clear his good name?

No. I am back to Bray
Wilkins and his lot. Swearing
he felt *in greivous pain & my water much stopt
till s'd Willard was in chains.*
Poor Willard hung, his great-greats
wronged, and me, if I were a witch,
I would put back the eyes, bring back
the boys who ran, and drown granddaddy
Bray in his own water.

Sonnets from the Marriage-Impaired:
 Eat at Your Own Table


For thirty years we have feasted only
on each other. Only my lips you kiss.
I lick one trail of coiled hair that slowly
leads to the known, the connubial bliss
that has faithfully fueled a lasting love.
We have munched our smorgasbord, and swallowed
days and weeks into years until full of
our God-approved, guilt-free nourishment. Bored
ordering the daily special, we crave
bacon, a peanut butter banana,
warm croissant, or juicy sausage to stave
the munchies after our dinner of manna
again. Stepping on the scale holds us back,
helps us weigh what we have, not what we lack.

## Casualties of War

*Fucking idiots* my husband spits, rants, aims
the remote at the Channel 7 talking head.
War news at 6 for supper, then at 10
*for Christ's sake can't you just say* dead?

Stew bubbles on the stove, potatoes, peas,
carrots waiting for the beef to turn tender.
Baking soda stirred with flour, kneaded,
and cut into rounds brown, offer surrender.

## Something Comes and Takes What We Don't Want

All day, leftovers get scraped into an old metal bowl next to the sink: burnt crusts of bread from breakfast, chips dropped on the floor, unidentifiable innards from a chicken roasted for dinner, onion skins, and the like, mix into a stew I take yards behind the house and dump in what my husband's mother called the sump. In the morning, the leavings are gone save for some odds and ends like wrenched-out lemon peels and potatoes gone to eyes and mush. I wonder what has come and gone in the night while we sleep in my husband's childhood room, his army men packed away in their cardboard footlocker, Hot Wheels still parked on shelves with Hardy Boy mysteries and Tom Swift adventures.

A week after Thanksgiving I emptied the fridge, discarding in three walks to the end of the gravel path—a turkey carcass, a wobbly lump of cranberry sauce, ham hocks I was saving for beans but forgot, and all the soft stuff in the crisper drawer. At first light, as I ran water into the coffee pot, I could see the dregs had been picked clean as if a posse of buffet bandits hit up a Western Sizzlin' after hours. What crosses the property lines to graze and gobble on what we don't want then tips in scat? I ask my husband: What comes so close at night that we don't see? *Maybe a possum, probably raccoons,* he muses, *I saw a fox down by the barn, fat and slick; he looked me right in the eye. Bold.* And now I'm worried for my cat who likes to sun behind the house. That night in bed my husband snores, while I read a brittle copy of *Tom Swift on the Border for Uncle Sam*, listening for the rustle of leaves and sharp teeth gnawing, and determining to throw garbage in the trash because if you give a critter an inch, well, you know.

## Battlefield Photographs

Deep in the cove, the trees fell. Last winter,
ice heavy, sick with fungus, or in spring,
rain unburied roots and the trees splintered
yards from our house with no one listening.
Laid out like a corpse on the moss and fern,
a Bur Oak softens, a sponge for wasps, bees,
and beetles. Reaching, a birch's roots spurn
the damp earth, exposing deep rot, disease.
No witness, at least not me, felt echoes
vibrate on drums, signals of storms or war.
The forest could fall, one by one, heroes
rushing battle lines, but I have no scar.
The destructions' remains absorbed by age
linger, paused in image, printed on page.

After Minié balls spun and wound their way
into flesh, after grapeshot spray savaged
through cotton and wool, after the midday
dead blocked Bloody Lane, after the ravaged
armies stopped, Gardner recorded a silent
Antietam on the surface of wet plates.
Through a scope lens, away from the violent
preface, a heap of gray and blue still waits.
The bodies seem ready to stack like cords
of wood. Dunker Church, a backdrop, a plain
flag of surrender waves its pockmarked boards.
What other scenery has seen war's slain?
Jungles and deserts where my soldiers die?
Coming home to stare at empty blue skies?

My father's letters from Vietnam held
folded onionskin messages printed
in capital letters as if he yelled
at us from over there. Snapshots hinted
at another life. Smiling black-haired boys,
captured by his Kodak Instamatic,
held his pistol and M16 like toys.
A life in motion, while we stayed static.
I printed the picture you emailed me,
The one where you're sitting, on Saddam's
throne. You said each soldier in the army
took a turn—a break from roadside bombs
that wait, anticipating your last breath.
No matter. I am deaf to trees and death.

# Work

I sit down to type, to write a poem,
maybe two, maybe a book of poems
in one day, a blog-poem-project,
but no words come, well, these words, but not
good ones, I know, so I go to walk
on our farm, where we live sometimes, where
my husband's mother was born, grew up,
in a house that caught fire. An uncle
burned leaves, the flames took control
until all that was left was the chimney,
ready for more wood.
I hike through the cultivated fields,
planted with winter wheat, ready
to cut so I make a mental note
to listen for the combines so I
can watch as they sweep over the land,
a mechanical army of troops
on their march again to the sea. I
walk into the woods, step sideways down
the banks into the coves where the sun
finds paths to light. I think, all of this
is a poem. I take a breath to calm
myself a bit, and that breath, my breath
here on the farm, all the breathing done
plowing fields, feeding a cow or mule
on cold mornings, all the work done not
exactly how I labor to make a poem,
this poem, but maybe, a little bit.

# Sonnets from the Marriage-Impaired:
## Share Troubles

When you speak, your bottom lip works free,
loosens into a tremble. A stern warning
spills over tender flesh, insists I see
danger. I watch your sweet mouth, ignoring
caution. I want to reach out and silence
the barrage of words you fire. Terrorists
who would slice through my neck. Violence
in places I don't know. I want to kiss
your mouth and stop the endless alarm
to lock the bolt keeping out those swearing
to hate, enemies seeming to mean us harm.
Not all is dire. Stop to rest. We are wearing
out from the daily fight against the apocalypse
uttered by the exposed unkissed edge of your lips.

# Petty Thefts

Last Saturday night, the Comanche County cops
arrested my nephew for stealing a fruitcake
at the Cache Road Walmart. Overmedicated
on medical marijuana, he was hungry.

When Dawn, his parole officer, sighed and asked why,
Davey just said it was about his grandmother.
When he's himself, not the person on whatever,
the man—not that young anymore—doesn't say much,

his stutter never ceased despite the years called out
of class. My sister says for him that he hankers
for our ma's—his granny's—fruitcake. Unrelated
to the brick of Claxton he ate in the store's aisles,

our ma baked early, studding Aunt Sue's recipe
she claimed her own with pecans pilfered from orchards
on Fort Sill's range, candied cherries and pineapple
bought on clearance at the end of the last season—

all chopped fine—no chunks to spit into a napkin.
She wrapped the cake in a linen dish towel, the one
commemorating Diana and Charles' failed
marriage, then poured Jameson over the top, sealed

it in foil, and hid it in a Stetson box, the one left
from Dad's summer hat, on a shelf in her closet.
Every Sunday, she unwrapped it, let us all whiff
the cake, fruit, and whiskey, then gave it another

drink and a wee one for the baker. When the twelve
days commenced, ma sliced slivers, the fruit translucent
like stained glass. This Christmas, I think I'll stir one up
for us all to share and one for Davey all his own.

## Hello, Leave a Message

Last night on the phone you said,
*No, you just don't care.*
I looked away from the television.
I was binge watching the last season
of *The Walking Dead*, scanning
Pinterest for Fourth of July pie while
I made the compulsory call.
*Hey baby, how's it going?* I asked.
Then the amnesia set in I suppose,
until, *No, you just don't care.*
What else did you say? Something
about how I don't listen, maybe. Or
was it the asshole at work who still
doesn't know your name? Or my brother
who doesn't care about my mom
or anyone else except his own fat self?
Then Rick and Michonne kick some zombie
ass, thrusting knives into the skulls
because that's the only way to kill
them, even chopping off their heads
doesn't work because the mouths
will just keep gaping, yammering
something, I think, about how no one
cares until I'm sick of this show,
just too tired to listen anymore.

## Rolling Along

Dad went to Vietnam to fight the Damn Communists.
His starched fatigues fell limp in the orange haze of the jungle
while flower-smocked Mom smoked Luckys, drank whiskey and TAB,
watched *Dark Shadows*, and read her magazine-dreams.

When Dad came home, she rolled her hair on juice cans,
wore crushed velvet hot pants, lined her lips with frosted
pink Tabu, then practiced a photograph pose in her compact.

*And those caissons go rolling along* except no Fourth of July
bottle rockets, no campouts at Beaver's Bend, no Sunday drives
in the Rambler, singing like congregants in a Baptist choir.

My husband went to Iraq to fight the Damn Terrorists.
His techno camo, boots, and Beretta choked in Saddam's sand
while I slept in sweats, piped classic rock through Apple earbuds,
sipped icy White Russians, and kept watch on eBay bids.

When he came home, I shaved my legs, bleached my brown hair
a Nice 'N Easy neutral blonde, raised breasts with underwire,
and smeared "I ♥ my soldier" in lipstick on the bathroom mirror.

*And those caissons go rolling along* except for the Xanax and Ambien
on the bedside table, the hours cursing the news, flat screen glowing
like an illumination round guiding a missile. *For it's hi, hi, hee*

in American history, in rent houses waiting for the thin blue letter,
the telephone ring, the email ping, because *you will always know* men
who fight come and go to women who stay and wait for the return home.

# Sonnets from the Marriage-Impaired:
## Take Your Time

A week before we pack and take a trip-
to visit our son, see the Fall leaves turn,
or stand in Times Square to watch the year slip
into the new-you warn me. Always stern,
you announce: *Departure, o-dark-thirty.*
A time which means, I think, six, or five.
As the day to go draws near, you decree
we must leave at four-thirty to arrive
by the hard deadline you set for us both.
I promise to be ready. Don't worry.
To ease your heart's tight springs, here's my oath:
I, your wife, solemnly swear to hurry.
Then when time stops, and you no longer live,
I will think of you who rushed in life, and forgive.

# The Elephant in the War

Bombs might set her free. Loose, conceivably
to ravage Belfast. So she, the tiger,
six wolves, one lynx, and a bear could not be
trusted out of cages, too much desire
to run amok. So they were all condemned
by the Ulster Constables to die at the zoo.
But a woman, an animal keeper friend
led the calf, Shelia, down a path into
her walled garden, far from the Blitz, beyond
attacks by the Luftwaffe and home guard.
Snapshots expose survival and the bond
between keeper and kept—all who are barred
and prisoners to the world at war and war
at home, no freedom anywhere anymore.

## Limits to Human Curiosities

Did Eng close his eyes? Did he read the paper when
Chang and Addie kissed, screwed, whispered
sweet words? Or did he cop a feel, again
compare breasts and thighs to big sister's?
Did Sally hate the other's moans? A damp,
cinderblock cellar below Sheriff Griffin's
playhouse, lit by buzzing fluorescent lamps,
displays "The Original Siamese Twins."
Photographs, scrawled letters, handbills, fixed
in dime store frames gossip to me. Fathers
to twenty-one children conceived betwixt
the two and two in one bed. These Others
I paid my fee to see, to gawk at the freak show—
me, a slack-jawed voyeur standing here below.

Me, the slack-jawed voyeur, who stands below
the hardwood joists, searches the men called Right
and Left for signs of separation, a cutting blow.
Games of cards? Too much drink? What began the fight
to life's end? Was it mutual rage at the band that linked
chest to chest, stretched like a paltry dinner
prepared for one, their hunger never extinct?
A clot, a random shared-blood-splinter,
stopped one heart. The dead half whispered, follow me
to a grave in Mount Airy's tourist trade. The sound
of mountain bluegrass and shows of human oddity
held a Mayberry sideshow underground.
I saw all the sights and exited to stinging light
exposed to the lust and loathing I unite.

## Persistent Suicide

My sister's husband keeps pouring her shots
from a handle of Powers 80 proof
stored on the coffee table, her own hand
too trembly, feet too swollen to totter
from the couch where she curls and sleeps
between rages shrieking she fucking hates
us all, assholes, all. My other sister
and I sit silent, nothing more to say,
and watch her down one after another.

I knew better

but nevertheless picked up a rock on a trail
near our house. No resisting the Oklahoma-
shaped-granite bedded in the dirt, so I reached down,

digging my bare fingers beneath the part that looked
like the panhandle. As I turned my state right side,
the Red River jagged at the bottom border,

a scorpion crawling right around Tulsa leapt,
I swear he leapt, reared his tail, and popped his venom
right on my left ring finger below the knuckle.

Hot agony shot through me like BBs ripping
through the tin roof I used to perfect my aim.
Like when my bell-bottoms pulled my bare ankle

into my bike's spokes as I cruised past Wacker's Drug,
like when who I loved did not love me back. I lost
control, flung the rock I wanted against other

rocks shattering the Sooner state into pieces
that could never be put back. I left the stones
where they landed and went home, somewhere else in the dirt.

# Eye Exam

I lean into the machine
and Dr. Head offers
choices. He clicks to A,
then to B. Which is better?

I say nothing. Both look
okay, the same. Perhaps
A appears sharper,
and B seems bigger,

I guess. No blood test,
no confirmation, just
one way or the other.
Take a side and live

with it. Vegan or meat?
Smoke a little weed?
Pack a pistol? Drive
a Prius or take the bus?

Say yes to the dress?
Allow the cells
in my womb to multiply?
Glasses or contacts?

He clicks again to A
then to B. I widen my stare,
will myself to know,
to bring the answers into focus.

*Excuse me, Mister Rooster Hat, you've crossed the line*

I want to say, but don't.
I want to elbow the encroacher
in the seventeen inches of padded plastic next to me,
raise the brim of his trucker cap,
point my mom-finger at COCK—embroidered in red,
and teach him some airline etiquette.
I want to put up a wall
between my 20A window seat
and his 20B seat on the aisle.
I want to pinch his gym-rat beefy arm
swallowing the three-inch armrest,
poke his thick thigh, sprawling, friendly-like,
as if we're a common law married couple
hanging out on the couch in our doublewide.
I want to stuff my neck pillow in his mouth,
stop the constant breeze of his breath,
a bit whiskey-soured, breaking past his full lips
in the regular rhythm of REM
as he cups his genitals in that defensive gesture
men assume in sleep, ready for a quick game
of slumber-rugby or a knee in the groin by a jilted girl.
I want to reach into his backpack, pull out
his dinging-ringing phone and slide into airline mode
so the plane doesn't spiral into a fiery crash.
I want to be kind, not scream: *COCK-A-DOODLE-DOO,
time for you to move!* I want to want to offer a shoulder,
listen as he tells me why he was drunk last night,
why he hasn't taken a shower, what the ink means:
the jagged currents, the single die landed on a snake eye,
the memorial of a woman stretched over a bicep
her face distorted, begging for a flex.
I want to understand his dream mumblings,
who are you calling and who is calling you?

## Lost in First Class

My husband upgrades my ticket, redeems
frequent flyer miles like my sharp mother
who traded books of S&H Green Stamps
for a pressure cooker that could tenderize
a pot roast in an hour. I flip through
the slick *American Way* magazine,
contemplate the menu: Grilled chicken glazed
with red wine reduction or a bleu cheese-
stuffed Portobello as the masses schlep
to coach like Dust Bowl migrants making
their way to a California that doesn't want
them. The flight attendant brings
me fresh juice and prosecco for mimosas,
sparkling water, crisp brown cookies,
warm nuts, pillow, blanket, and the *New York Times*.
Wizards work behind the accordion curtain,
keep separate the riff from raff, the public from private,
the hoi polloi from haunt monde like cowboys
culling sick cows. At descent,
I receive the flight's final offering,
a steamy square dropped by tongs into my
sticky, itchy palms. I wipe my hands clean,
gather my carry-on and contemplate
making our dinner without the pressure
and prizes earned, just in regular time.

# Sonnets from the Marriage-Impaired:
## Spend Time Together

After I wash my hair, I twist it up
tight into a towel or old white T-shirt
to dry. I apply lotion and make-up,
listen to Merle Haggard's concert
*Live at Billy Bob's.* My husband calls down
the hall: *Need to leave in five minutes.*
My fogged mirror turns turban into crown
and if I were queen there would be no limits
to the time I linger in the bathroom steam
instead of going out with friends I don't know.
Baby, open the door and enter my dream
where Merle croons low, *going where the lonely go.*
Live here in my kingdom beside the sink
and I vow *to care about what* you *think.*

## Local Traffic

The Dollar General next
to the Gentlemen's Club, across
from Love's on HWY 44, now stocks
Blue Bell, which as you know
if you have ever heard the jingle
played on Southern stations, once made
the best ice cream in the country.
As a person who eats her share
of ice cream I agree, it's tasty,
the Homemade Vanilla rich with fake essence.
The folks down in Brenham churned
out half gallons and once, only down
in Texas could I stop the cravings.
In that place, I ate my fill
after two-stepping with cowboys
at the Broken Spoke, my thumb caught
in belt loops, my boots sliding
in sawdust, and always taking
one home for the night
like a rented carpet cleaner.
Alvin Crow and the Pleasant Valley Boys
ended sets by crooning Blue Bell,
the best ice cream in the country
and then Al would pull his fiddle
from under his chin and yodel.
But that was years before
distribution widened and the Broken
Bow, Oklahoma factory sent us
into Listeria and I still fed
my addictions with the good stuff.
Now, it's convenient when urges set in
and I'm jonesing for a fix and considering a cruise
down to the other place where I was
and left, that our local Dollar General,
carries pints to eat at home while I listen
to "80s Country" on Pandora and wait
until I hear a clear *yodelayheehoo*
to broadcast past the static
on pickup truck FM radios
still hurtling down my rural roads.

## Love-Hate Contract

If you love me, hate who I hate:
the bitch at work who rolls
her Purie eyes when I'm late,
the guy in the Prius that extols
his great environmental virtue
then parks in my space. Hitler,
well that's a given, a few
characters from Bible scripture
like Herod who killed two-year-
olds. Cain, the jealous brother,
Judas—hate—that seems clear.
Who else? I'm sure there are others.
For love's sake! Just hate who I hate,
there's the dotted line, share the weight.

Here's the dotted line, share this weight.
Plus, always love me best. Choose
your affections, but, do not allocate
love, even like, for any woman who's
beyond first cousin. Please love
your mother. Listen to her endless
list: arthritic knees, clogged bowels, talk of
church, and who attended.
Love our son, of course. Like Hitler hate,
that's a given. Love the loser Cowboy football
team and your Aggie Corps roommate.
Oh, just love who I love, no one else at all.
Your true passions reveal your heart,
knowing their direction, always smart.

## The Magically Lucky Ones

A round of white phosphorus lit acres
of thirsty grass on Fort Sill's range where
the artillery practices for war,

and so fast, like turning your back
in Walmart and losing a child
the fire lost control,

began to rage, leapt across hills, firebreaks,
then Boundary Road and HWY 49
into Medicine Park where it swallowed

up a trailer park and all that grew:
scrub oaks, prickly pear and barrel cacti
in bloom. Volunteer firemen from town led

by Chief McCoy, and men from other towns
like Paradise Valley and Apache
tried to hush her screams with sprays of water

that fell on the heat like cool cloths on
a febrile babies. After three days, the fire just
tuckered out.

The house across Big Rock Road where we live
was a twisted rag and our house was okay.
We say, "We were so fortunate that day."

In my Walmart, I rushed up and down the aisles,
fluorescents buzzing, and I called my boy
who stood quiet, gazing up at the boxes

of cereal. I let him buy Lucky
Charms, all sugar and artificial color,
I was that happy I could take him home.

## O, Mothers, Where Art Thou?

My son, who is writing a thesis on the intersection of statistics, media, and man-called to discuss the condition of the asparagus in his Frigidaire crisper drawer. *I bought it last Friday at Trader Joe's. Today I opened the cellophane bag and found moisture beaded on the still crisp spears—the buds are open. The smell is earthy.* Last week he called, across two time zones, needing a diagnosis: *a strange rash erupted, and forgive me Mom, on my scrotal sac.*

In a hot May, my belly heavy, I dreamed I closed him in a dresser drawer filled with old linen. At school, I taught *Macbeth* to high school seniors stuck to desks waiting for the bell. Days later I remembered my poor suckling babe, his boneless gums shriveled, tucked into tablecloths and doilies, his face aged like a raisin picked out of a cinnamon bun.

A week early I tried to force him out: stop, now push, now stop, until his head lodged in my birth canal like the Weird Sisters' chant: *Fair is foul and foul is fair*—an endless loop worming in my bashed brain.

Just where are Shakespeare's mothers? Macduff's ma with her ripped womb? Did Lear's wife take off with some Fuller brush man to leave him and his daughter devotion? The mothers that enter and exit are missing still. Gertrude in the closet? Lady Capulet and her silent treatment?

I want to research and write a thesis on William's mother issues and this crossroads where I'm left to assure a son to eat the spears, earthy is good, and perhaps it's just prickly heat.

## Volunteers

An oily black seed dropped
by a magpie, buried
by a feeder-raiding
squirrel, or whirled by wind,
hibernated for months
in the front flower bed
of our Fort Sill quarters,
then woke and exploded.

After supper, summer
nights, Dad and I unspooled
the hose, set the sprinklers,
checked our sunflower's growth,
measured the whiskered stalk,
monitoring mothers
notching doorjamb inches,
admiring progress.

At 7 p.m. sharp,
the on-duty MPs
waved from their patrol car,
post's parade Grand Marshalls
on a maneuver through
Artillery Village,
the daily inspection.
Dad saluted, muttered

*pricks*. Code violations:
lawns too long, bald patches,
trash cans left on the drive,
and "Weeds of Any Kind"
earned citations, warnings
to cut the grass or chop
down wildflowers. Protests
to protect our feral

Helianthus, its face
following the swelter
of Oklahoma's sun,
annoyed Dad's commander,
entertained my mother,
and allowed Dad and me
a common enemy,
who denied our weedy beauty.

# The Curse

Days ended with supper, bath, now I lay me down, and a fierce hiss to *go to sleep*—as if that command cast a spell like the apple in Snow White. Immune to the incantations of mothers, I listened for the steady exhalation of breath from my baby sister in the bottom bunk. The murmur of voices floating upstairs and down hallways mingled with a sliver of light under the door—a signal that moms, dads, aunts, and uncles drank coke mixed with whiskey, smoked Marlboros, sang the old songs, and told stories about the troubles back home. Girls in bed, or girls at all, slipped into tomorrow, forgotten once my tired mother put them to bed. But I refused sleep as well as the good advice hurled in her anger and frustration—*stay away from that boy, stand up straight, brush that hair*—and crept across the wooden floor and down the polished steps. Aware of my shadow and how it revealed me, I sat against the wall, my knees drawn up into my nightgown. My mother sang "She's Just a Bird in a Gilded Cage"—the song that made my father blow his nose into his pocket hankie and my Aunt Nora murmur, *Ah Kathleen, not that grim tale.* Her perfect voice formed the words in the melody she learned from her mother, *'Tis sad when you think of her wasted life.* I already knew the end as I turned and escaped into the darkness, the screen door slamming behind me. As I flew, I thought of my sister and regretted that I left her there, but she asked questions like *Where are we going?* and cried when Daddy, the merciful huntsman, swatted our backsides, hauled us back to bed and implored *For the love of God, please go to sleep before she comes back up here.*

# Dress for Success

    after Robert Frost

There's something in my clothes
that doesn't love to fasten,
to stay closed and keep in
what should be. My buttons loosen
from jackets, hang on by single threads,
then drop like acorns and leave my chest
defenseless against the cold,
to the wind that swells the back
like a superheroes cape, taut in route
to save the doomed city.
The zippers on my skirts splay apart
like flowers too long in the vase.

When today began, all seemed okay,
but somewhere in the halls or classrooms,
the fabric in my shirt began to reject
the form some seamstress stitched
in a factory, chatting with other women
in a language I have never known,
but can almost hear—the whir
of the sewing machines still echoing
in my shirt when it pops open
at the late meeting, the snaps tired
from holding the edges together for hours.
I cross my arms to remedy the gap
and colleagues infer anger, some attitude
of disgust. And, I am annoyed, so roll my eyes
just as my boss makes her latest command,
"Lock your private files." And, I do want to keep
my personal drawers secure, but there's something
in my clothes that doesn't love to close.

# Still Life

Here, on the Chinese chest, the collected sorrys—stacked notes, letters, cards—a ragged block tied with a white grosgrain ribbon, frayed at the ends, a scrap from a birthday package, and a black and white snapshot of him in uniform: Eisenhower jacket, four-in-hand, side cap dipping into his forehead, Leica camera strung around his neck, his Brownie gripped in his left hand. The photographer staring into another's lens standing next to a field, somewhere in Georgia.

Sometime, years from now, a grandchild may untie the ribbon or perhaps just the lady who arranges a lifetime on table for strangers to barter over: "Will you take two dollars?" The cards will open and the saved words, thoughts, prayers, sympathy, the Hallmark condolences that rolled down a conveyer belt at a drugstore or Walmart next to gallons of milk or a bottle of Aleeve, will recollect the loss of a husband, who stood on a road, camera ready.

# Sonnets from the Marriage-Impaired:
## Answer to Many Names

From somewhere in the house your voice will
call me: *Bunny!* You cannot find a book
left open, your pen tucked in a page. Look
next to the bed, or in the covers still
tossed and twisted from last night's chill
dreams where peace and sleep forsook.
You mumbled: *My wife.* The miss smiled and took
missus, forevermore a ma'am. Grown. Still
late at night, your breath whispers: *Baby.*
In your mind, who am I? One day the *Bitch*
who doesn't listen? Then your *Soul Mate?*
Am I the thing my Adam names? Maybe
all. The moods and desires flip the switch,
belong to both, and all we do is wait.

## Gone to America

*for a few wet weeks and you're back, sounding like a Yank.*
Hunched over a pint at the Coq & Bull, the man cut
his eyes in our direction. My ma spit back, *I'll thank
you, Paddy, to keep your words to yourself.* She shut
her mouth, tight, and held my Uncle Billy's arm so he
wouldn't leap over the table and take the man by the neck.
In Oklahoma, friends would come to our house for tea,
to hear my ma, her statements rising like questions. *Wee
bun for ya? Ach, go on?* My uncles in the states
shrugged their slumped shoulders at her, sucked back
tobacco juice, dabbed at bald heads, nodded to me to translate.
*Eejits,* she snarled, *Need a kick up the arse and a smack
in the gub.* My mother's voice a tangle of her here and home
in a battle to claim turf where tongues can hold their own.

## How I Learned American History

Name a reason colonists came to America. Study guide
in hand, I tutored my Irish mother. She ironed sun-dried

laundry: linen dishtowels, baby rompers, Dad's army green
fatigues, flowered housedresses, pleated school skirts, clean

white blouses with Peter Pan collars. *I'll tell you why I'm here,*
she snaps, leaning into the iron, *a tall Yank whisperin' in my ear.*

They came for freedom, ma. *Freedom, aye, they got poverty.*
*Next question.* How can citizens participate in their democracy?

Steam rises, twisting my mother's red hair, flushing her skin. *Vote.*
That's right ma; you're right on that one. *Yes, vote for dopes*

*and divils. Another*, she smiles. Name two rights in the Declaration
of Independence. She sets the iron on its heel. *Jefferson, a brazen*

*one, he is.* The holes spit water. *He and his lot can feck off. Two*
*rights yer ma got from bleeding America or my GI husband is you*

*wee chiselers and stacks of damp diapers.* She stretches pants across
the rickety board and we both forget the tests and all she lost.

# For the Pie-Anxious on Thanksgiving

Mrs. Smith bakes a fine pie and if you
have come to depend upon her, no shame
on you. The boxes of frozen Homestyle
Flavor, stacked behind the glass freezer doors
in the Walmart Supercenter promise
easy Thanksgiving tradition. You could
even lever it out of the tin, slip
the block in Grandma's depression glass plate
saved for the year you might have time to bake.
She wrote it out for you, Foolproof Flaky
Crust, on a lined recipe card. Her name
in the *From the kitchen of* blank. Halted
penmanship of failing health urges you
to keep her secrets. It's not hard. I'll tell
you things she didn't write, the parts she thought
you knew. No need for the Internet's help,
no Pioneer Woman's farm song-and-dance,
or food processors. Here's the truth:
Pie crust looks like it's all going all wrong
before it goes right. Scissor the Crisco
into the flour and salt using butter knives.
Leave some bigger lumps. Toss ice water
by tablespoons. Here's where it starts. You get
anxious. It won't hold together. Just dump
it on the counter. Take the heel of your
hand and push. See the streaks of white? Good. Scrape
it up with a spatula. Keep the faith.
Dust it with some flour. Begin to roll
with her rolling pin. It's probably at the back
of the cabinet with the canisters.
Just go for it. You don't need a perfect
circle. Roll thin if you can. You'll get holes.
It will stick to the counter. Expect it.
Again with the spatula, unstick what
you can. Urge it into the pan. Patch tears.
Pinch the edges into pleats. Or just let
them hang over the side. You can trim it later.
No matter what, you can cover
broken bits with whirls of Reddi Wip
or you can beat your own sweet
cream. It's easy and good. Find the mixer.

## I Believe All the Marys

With only one set of exams to grade, just two days
before Winter Holidays, I sit with my friend
in the teachers' lounge, graze on cut-out cookies
delivered by high school girls who have learned
to be nice to the teachers, and plates of cold-cuts
left by PTA moms who complain about reading lists.
We exchange worries: kids who sleep in class
or come back from lunch so stoned you get a contact high
when they stand too close in the hall, rattling off a story
about *this dude I know*. I multi-task: listen,
add anecdotes, and address Christmas cards
to my aunts, sliding in a photo from last summer—
my husband, son, and me holding sparklers on the fourth.
My friend tells me the components of the classic
sparkler are magnesium, sulfur, and potassium nitrate.
She teaches AP Chemistry to the college-bound, so she knows
these things, and I teach English II to sophomores
who sometimes can't read. She picks up a card, studies it.
I bought them at Hallmark at the end of last year, not my first choice,
but I knew my Aunt Norah would like to see baby Jesus
with his doting parents and the donkey looking down on him.
*You know that's a ridiculous story, right? An invention?*
my friend asks. I have to ask back, *What story?* because I was trying
to remember what's in a sparkler as if I could whip some up
like a pound cake. *The virgin birth*, she says. *A Roman soldier
fathered Jesus.* I have always liked men in uniform so I could
understand, and I have known some women who told
hard-to-swallow tales about babies conceived in hot tubs or spooning
naked, and, believe this or not, my extended family has used up
the national failure rate for birth control pills, which is 0.3 percent
for perfect use, and 9 percent for typical use, but I know the girls
in my family to be exceptional. *Mary made it all up?* I ask.
*Invented angels, whispered dreams in Joseph's ear, told her kid
he was the son of God?* My friend looks at me with some pity.
She's not unkind, and says, *No, of course not. Men wrote
the story to parallel other miraculous birth mythologies.*
And I think that few men I know would go that far to help
a woman out of a tough spot, but your gods have to come
from somewhere I suppose, so I study Mary's face and wish
I were in that barn, telling Mary, *I got your back* and waving
a homemade sparkler to celebrate the miracles we choose.

# Happy Birthday, Dear Helen

Each year on my sister's birthday, we eat
dinner at Red Lobster. We crack brittle
bumpy shells of crab legs, suck the sweet, white meat
until the skeletons empty, little by little.
On Helen's eighteenth, we clinked glasses.
Mom toasted: *My darling daughter is grown,
now a woman.* Dad tapped his cigar, the ashes
grown gray and dead. He stood, said, *Let's go home.*
On the drive, I watched Dad's silent detour toward
the Greyhound station where ladies strolled
and plied the daylight trade. He slowed the Ford,
rolled down the window. *I want you to know*, he told
us, *that girls marry men before they share their bed
or else they end up here, passed around, better off dead.*

## Weathered Men

Gathered in Oklahoma small town squares,
old men clinch cold cigars between bought teeth,
forecast, and broadcast sidewalk crops. Heirs
to white-wooden benches, thrones settled beneath
pecan shade trees planted for pie, they show
respect to ladies, tip Stetsons, ask for
weather reports: *Cold enough for ya? Blow
hard enough last night? Suspect y'll need more
rain down your way? Been dry?* They look up toward
the sky, conjure old-bone spirits: *Sure feels
like snow in my joints.* They give advice: *Bored
with the weather, wait an hour.* They make deals:
*I beg you, Lord, send rain to earth I've seeded,
and on Earth's dry places where we need it.*

*On the Earth's dry places where we need it,*
thunders a preacher, soft palms raised, *Repent!*
Farmers sit in tent revivals, cheated
into believing a bargain: Time spent
working soil and praying for rain wields
a fair fate. Sweat-stained hats in hands,
thirsty for faith in God and red dirt fields
—homesteads staked on old Indian lands,
borders redrawn over lines in the dust,
the sinners watch flocks of women begin
to sway, whisper amens, and ask for trust
in their menfolk to turn away from sins
planted in nights when wind ripples and rolls
canvas walls, rising the grit of lost souls.

## Sometimes We Remember What's Hard to Forget

My sister crawls into my bed, forces me
to scoot closer to the wall, face-to-face
with a glossy of Charlie Sheen's brother
in *The Breakfast Club*. She twists her cold feet
into the hem of my flannel nightdress,
drapes her arm over my back, and zigzags
her fingers into mine. Her damp hair smells
like the strawberry shampoo I hid in the cabinet
behind the extra towels so I say, *Go back
to your own bed. There's no room for you.*
And, it is true that our matching twin beds separated
only by a strip of shag carpet and a white wicker table
with her side and mine, are meant for one,
but she is small and doesn't take up too much space.
She says my name, but I don't answer.
She keeps saying my name until I say, *What?*
a game we have always played.
*I was in Bicycle Park,* she whispers and I know
it wasn't on her old Schwinn.
*Scott and I were talking and some other stuff,*
she keeps telling me. And then she's crying.
I turn and ask, *What's the matter? Did he hurt
you?* She nods no and tells me a policeman shined a light
into Scott's car, told her to go wait in his cruiser.
She told me she did. First, he jerked up Scott.
Then he slid in next to my little sister, said she could
do for him what she was doing for her boyfriend
and he'd let her go free—wouldn't tell our dad or take her
and Scott to the station. And then we're both crying.
Our faces touch like twins in our mother's womb,
but her turn was years after mine so I stroke her fresh
hair, and keep telling her to *forget it, just forget it.*

*Fine*

She says and glances
through the square window
at the train rolling
bumbling, rumbling past.
Her eyes, rimmed in gray
shadow, twisted clouds.
Her skin, pocked with lumps
erupting with pus.
Her bottom lip chewed
into a sore pulp
like the loose oozing
entrails of a possum
lost to headlights on
two-lane coal asphalt.
Her heaving breath soured
by Pall Malls and Jack,
a wailing exhaust
steaming and screeching
on the rails of *fine*.

# The Cuckoo Order of Birds

In the strip between the asphalt
and scrub oaks, a roadrunner
forages spring's bluestem grass.
He wears his Mohawk and cobalt
eye liner like a small-town teenage
girl annoying a Baptist grandmother.
The bird performs an impatient
dance, flitting across rocks, revealing prey:
a beetle, crickets, a plague
of grasshoppers, and a tiny gray mouse
that he batters against a granite altar
until its bowels, exposed and useless,
are sucked down, filling a restless need.

# No Escape from the Good Deed of the Day

Today, help arrives at the Dollar General in Medicine Park. Stacked boxes of Thin Mints, Samosas, and Trefoils—teetering pyramids piled on card tables—block the sidewalk. Shoppers dodge and weave through a maze of wading pools, bags of Kingsford charcoal, and the Polar Bear ice machine while Brownies nip at their heels—miniature barkers at the impromptu carnival: *Cookies! $3.50 a box!* Uniformed scouts, a prepubescent army equipped with factory baked goods, bum rush old men jonesing for Lucky Strikes, redneck boys scoring Miller Lite, and the night-shift Goodyear tire makers stopping for Cheetos and Mountain Dew. Hordes of little girls push sugary sustenance, just one Do-Si-Do around the dance floor. Suppliers ring up sales. A Quartet chants, *Camp!* where legions make sit-upons, hobo stew, and lanyards. Troop 14, green sashes worn like pageant wannabes, hold doors, in and out, prospecting for the soft touch, change not yet pocketed. *Forty-two more boxes and I'll earn my badge.* An emissary tails me and I step quick, avoid her reminder, *Get the Tagalongs before we run out.* I mumble, *Tomorrow.* Her eyes turn to slits and she hisses through gapped teeth, *I'll be here all week.*

# There's this

chimney standing roadside as commuters hurry
to swivel in desk chairs for hours times hour.
When work inhales light, they turn and scurry
back on black asphalt again past the prairie tower
abandoned to trespassers in papery nests. Stones
exhumed from Oklahoma clay hold together still.
A city-gone son interred his father, left the bones
of the last man to mud the granite's gaps, to till
the stubborn fields, to harvest grain, to hold
a homestead. Twigs gathered but never kindled,
the chimney casts only cold shadows. Long gone mold-
skimmed walls milled from scarce oak dwindled
into pyramids of dust until only the rock remains
of a flame that once sustained life on these plains.

# Fighters Fight

A bigger girl on the school bus kept after me.
Jerks on the braid dangling down my back,
her leg a gate across the aisle, bus driver

shouting, *Sit your ass down!* Now, I don't know
why. Maybe the boy she liked liked me
or maybe because the English teacher kept me

as a pet and the kids who couldn't conjugate
liked to rattle my cage. One day in May, I leapt
from the bus. My dad waited on our porch,

a cigarillo clinched between his teeth. He waved
and my brain pounded I run, you run, he/she/
or it runs! The girl shouted after me, *Go*

*home to your old goat of dad.* A fight filled
my throat like liver I couldn't swallow
even after hours at the table unexcused.

I pounced on her, twisted fists of hair, and levered
my all, pounded her head into the soft-spring ground,
mashed her face into the new grass. My dad fought

a war through North Africa up through Sicily
where he ". . . traded for a small native boy
who had no parents and was half starved. The little waif

wore a sheep's skin when [Dad] first got him, wrapping
it around him so his arms and legs were where the legs
of the sheep had been." A brittle clipping

from *The Broken Bow News* my Aunt Sue kept
folded in her bible said the boy ". . . has fleshened
up and is learning to talk English a little."

I'd read the words, "He intends to bring the boy back
when he returns," over and over, and asked
my dad where the boy was now, but he didn't know

how that story ended. After two more wars, he fought
young GIs who flirted with my pretty mother
in the NCO club. *Ah Sarge, he meant no disrespect.*

He parted the circle of kids, lifted me off the girl,
held my flailing arms, his ragged voice cooing,
*You've had enough.* I did not want to fight.

I take detours. Avoid bullies. Skip
on my own street. Until the moment
someone calls my old man a goat.

## Arrangements

Somewhere between the kitchen bar, Easy
Go, and Huddle's Funeral Home, my sister
got drunk. She parked her car next to mine, sucked

spiked diet Coke from a Styrofoam cup,
and her glazed eyes gave her away. *Christ*, I
thought, *here we go*. No point in coaxing her

to stay behind, shaming her DNA,
rehab reruns, or our Irish mother's
disappointment, so I took her hand and led

her inside the cool dark where another
sister swayed on the foyer's red shag like
an aging ingénue caught cruising bad

neighborhoods for weed. Click, paparazzi.
The undertaker and his wife—always
a family affair this business—led us

away from the chapel to the office.
*So sorry for your loss. Cup of coffee?*
My drunk sister browsed bookshelves, overturned

mementoes looking for value as if
browsing a swap meet. I wrote a check
for the down payment, the showroom entry fee

to the Costco of caskets. My swaying
sister stumbled between coffins, pressing
her hands into satin, fingering price

tags like a timid teenager trolling
the Buick dealer. She wanted the white
Cadillac with Crucifix tailfins. *Not*

*that one,* I whispered, *Ma was an Irish
Prod, for Christ's sake.* My drunk sister
began yanking at the silver-plated cross

to customize the coffin. She grabbed
lifeless Jesus in her fist, twisted
Him until He broke free and sent her

stumbling backward, holding our dear Lord
and Savior above her head like
a home run ball caught in the upper

deck. We froze in a fairground sideshow
tableau vivant. My mother's voice
pounded in my head, *Don't be a fool*

and I wondered if I should haggle
the price of damaged goods or just run.

## Toasted on Toasts with the Good Stuff

I've popped the cork.

    The champagne archived,

        now

  sipped, swigged, guzzled,

     gone

  to a craving for bubbles,

      orbs

of fading suds in a lukewarm

    bath.

  I've poured out prospects.

The bottle hoarded

    once,

  waited, like a patient, finally

    called

  from the back of the Frigidaire

     chilled

from the wait next to the crusty catsup and

    scraps

of suppers in Petri dish Tupperware.

I tossed back shots of sweetness.

    The prize that lingered for

        toasts

to friends in love: Here's to

    you.

A baby swaddled, Here's to

    him.

A house mortgaged, Here's to

    us.

    A diploma earned, Here's to

        me.

I tipped all down my gullet.

    Emptied into the bottomless

    ocean

of my gut, gone, and worth the

    waste.

## Sonnets from the Marriage Impaired:
### Cease Fires before You Say What Can't Be Forgotten

The gorilla at the Washington DC Zoo
catapulted quick across her terrain,
beat her sagging breasts and eyeballed me through
the glass that seemed too fragile to contain
her rage. "She really hates you," my husband
said smiling. "Why?" I asked, "I've done nothing."
The glass vibrated as the gorilla made demands
I didn't understand, mouthing something
heard in memory, "You're not capable
of love." Years ago, we warred. Why? Now,
I don't know—but, partners, both blamable.
And, though your words incited years ago,
they recall in me a need to end a fight,
place open hands against my breast, just quiet.

# Escape Routes Wait in the Woods

"Watch out for abandoned wells,"
my husband's mother warns me.
I tie up my boots, itchy
for a wander in the woods
where one day I might plunge
down that hole she said I would.

Maureen Oehler DuRant's cousin in Broken Bow, Oklahoma died last year at 102, yet her Aunt Mary in Belfast, Northern Ireland lives on and turns 100 in April, so she believes, perhaps, there is still time, after all, to be a poet. Maureen earned an MFA in Creative Writing with her patient husband's GI Bill at Queens University of Charlotte and her poetry has appeared in *Crosstimbers, Red River Review, Westview,* and *The Great American Wise Ass Poetry Anthology.* She is the co-author of *Postcard History Series: West Point,* published by Arcadia Press, 2007. She currently serves as the country's loudest librarian at Lawton High School and teaches at Cameron University.

www.ingramcontent.com/pod-product-compliance
Lightning Source LLC
LaVergne TN
LVHW041344080426
835512LV00006B/609